G000166285

FIVE FOLK - SONGS

arranged for unaccompanied mixed voices

by DAVID WILLCOCKS

for Annabel

1. THE LASS OF RICHMOND HILL

Poem by W. UPTON   *Melody by* JAMES HOOK

*or group of baritones.

© Oxford University Press, 1975

Oxford University Press, Music Department, 44 Conduit Street, London, WIR 0DE

Printed in Great Britain

2

4

6

Hill; Rich — mond Hill,

Hill; Rich — mond Hill,

Hill; Rich — mond Hill,

Hill; of Rich - mond Hill, of Rich - mond Hill,

Hill;

Hill; of Rich - mond Hill, of Rich - mond Hill,

Rich — mond Hill.

Rich — mond Hill.

Rich — mond Hill.

sweet lass.

sweet lass.

sweet lass.

Five Folk-Songs

for David

2. BARBARA ALLEN

Old English

If preferred, accompanying parts may be sung to *Ah,* or hummed, in some verses.

8

Verses 3 & 5

Five Folk-Songs

Verses 4 & 6

10

Repeat for verse 5

3. DRINK TO ME ONLY

Words by BEN JONSON

Traditional English

Words in italics may be sung to *Ah,* or hummed.

12

Five Folk-Songs

Five Folk-Songs

1.

would ___ not change for ___ thine, change for thine.

would ___ not change for thine. ___

would ___ not change for thine. ___

would not change ___ for thine, change for thine.

would ___ not change for thine. ___

2.

of ___ it - self, but ___ thee. Drink, ___ drink, drink.

of ___ it - self, but thee. Drink, ___ drink, drink.

of ___ it - self, but thee. ___

of it - self, ___ but thee. Drink, ___ drink, drink.

of ___ it - self, but thee. Drink, ___ drink, drink.

for Michael

4. EARLY ONE MORNING

Old English

16

Verse 4

Five Folk-Songs

Five Folk-Songs

for Robin

5. BOBBY SHAFTOE

Traditional English

Five Folk-Songs

20

Five Folk-Songs

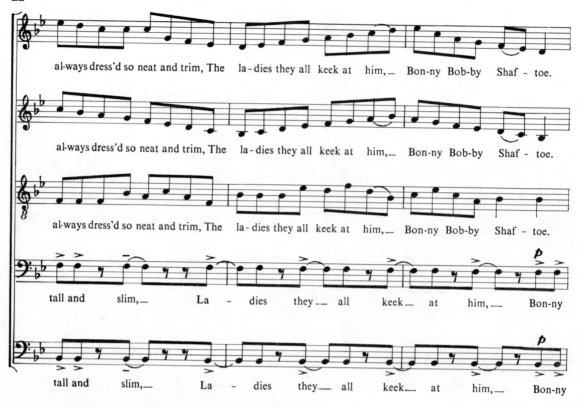

al-ways dress'd so neat and trim, The la-dies they all keek at him,__ Bon-ny Bob-by Shaf-toe.

al-ways dress'd so neat and trim, The la-dies they all keek at him,__ Bon-ny Bob-by Shaf-toe.

al-ways dress'd so neat and trim, The la-dies they all keek at him,__ Bon-ny Bob-by Shaf-toe.

tall and slim,__ La - dies they__ all keek__ at him,__ Bon-ny

tall and slim,__ La - dies they__ all keek at him,__ Bon-ny

Bob-by Shaf-toe's get-ten a bairn, For to dan-dle in his arm, In his arm and on his knee,

Bob-by Shaf-toe's get-ten a bairn, For to dan-dle in his arm, In his arm and on his knee,

Bob-by Shaf-toe's get-ten a bairn, For to dan-dle in his arm, In his arm and on his knee,

Five Folk-Songs

Five Folk-Songs